Aberdeenshire Library and Information Service
www.aberdeenshire.gov.uk/libraries
Renewals Hotline 01224 661511

IC

– 6 NOV 2009

1 0 MAR 2010

3 0 MAR 2012

1 8 OCT 2014

2 4 FEB 2017

1 2 FEB 2018

MAR 18.

– 1 FEB 2020

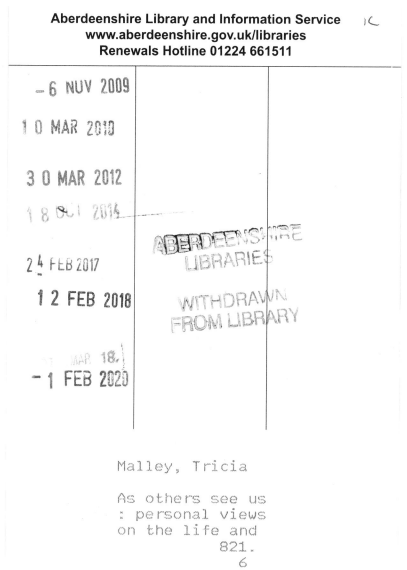

ABERDEENSHIRE
LIBRARIES

WITHDRAWN
FROM LIBRARY

Malley, Tricia

As others see us
: personal views
on the life and
      821.
        6
1846073

D0504814

The photographers

Award winning photographers Ross Gillespie and Tricia Malley, collectively known as broad daylight, are among Scotland's most experienced and insightful photographers. Having worked together for almost 20 years they have an instinctive eye for capturing the character and personality behind their subjects. Tricia's background as a documentary photographer combined with Ross's background as an illustrator has created a collaboration which allows art to frequently and successfully mimic life in a seriously powerful fashion.

They have produced several major bodies of portraiture work, one of which features some of Scotland's most influential power brokers. They have an enormous capacity for empathy with their subjects and as a result get well beyond the superficial. Their portraits tell more than just the immediate story and their work is in the collections of both the Scottish National Portrait Gallery in Edinburgh and the National Portrait Gallery in London.

Their attraction to Scotland's gritty underbelly led to commissions for the evocative front covers for Ian Rankin's Rebus novels and a semi-autobiographical picture book entitled *Rebus's Scotland*... broad daylight simply understands that a picture can tell more than a thousand words.

www.broaddaylightltd.co.uk

AS OTHERS SEE US
is supported by:

Homecoming Scotland

Clyde Blowers

FirstGroup Plc

The Leith Agency

broad daylight

Hasselblad

Bowens

Holyrood Magazine

The Scottish Government

Professor Walter Nimmo

Professor David W Purdie and friends

Alan McFarlane

Margaret H Duffy

Michael Staniland

In association with

The Scottish National Portrait Gallery

Luath Press

The Scottish Parliament is a partner
in AS OTHERS SEE US

Tricia and Ross would like to
thank the following for their advice,
assistance and patience in producing
AS OTHERS SEE US:

John K McGregor; Margaret H Duffy;
Mrs M Gillespie; Marjory and Ian Clyde;
Mandy Rhodes; Christine Mullin; Ross
Hunter, Joe and Tweeter; Focus
Management; Joanne Deponio at
Homecoming Scotland; Professor James
McGonagle; Pam Heaton; Scottish
Opera; Gordon Boag and John at
Kelvingrove Art Gallery and Museum;
Jane Skinner at Secret Music; Paul
Rigby, Andy and the team at Palacerigg
Country Park; Reverend James Gibson at
Bothwell Parish Church; Glasgow
Botanic Gardens; Abode Hotel Glasgow;
Fiona McDougall, Roy Devon and Alan
Rennie at The Scottish Parliament;
Christian Howes; Shepperton Studios;
Avril Gill and Emma Low of FirstGroup
Plc; Angela Sharkey of Clyde Blowers;
Brian Coane, Bob Lovie, Nic Siegel and
Alan Ainsley of The Leith Agency;
Linda Fabiani MSP; Ben Boswell and
Paul Waterworth at Hasselblad; Gavin
MacDougall at Luath Press; Hamish
Barrie; Scott Porter; Graeme Sturroch;
John and Frank at Peter Howson's
studio; Julie Lawson and James
Holloway at The Scottish National
Portrait Gallery.

Burns texts collated by Professor
David W Purdie.

And finally... all the sitters for their time,
patience and co-operation.

AS OTHERS SEE US is part of the
Homecoming 2009 celebrations

AS OTHERS SEE US

Personal views on the life
and works of Robert Burns

Portraits by
Tricia Malley and Ross Gillespie

Luath Press Limited

EDINBURGH

www.luath.co.uk

First published 2009

ISBN: 978-1-906817-06-0

The paper used in this book is recyclable. It is made
from low chlorine pulps produced in a low energy,
low emissions manner from renewable forests.

Printed and bound by Scotprint, Haddington

Typeset in 8.5 point Helvetica Neue and
Kings Caslon Display

Design by The Leith Agency

Robert Burns by Alexander Nasmyth on page 10
reproduced courtesy of The Scottish National
Portrait Gallery

© Tricia Malley and Ross Gillespie 2009
www.broaddaylightltd.co.uk
contact by email: info@broaddaylightltd.co.uk

Malley, Tricia

As others see
us : personal
views on the
                      821.
                        6
1846073

Burns showed me that there was a place for me on this earth – as well as for Caesar...
John Young, Shoemaker, at the Burns Centenary, 1859

His poems and songs, first laid before his family in the farmlands of Ayrshire, were to become the property and the patrimony – of Mankind'
Professor David W Purdie

Contents

Foreword

Robert Burns, Scotland's National Bard, has an unrivalled place in the affections of the people of Scotland. He is also known all over the world. His birthday on 25 January is celebrated at Burns suppers, and the words of his poem 'Auld Lang Syne' are sung in a spirit of reconciliation and friendship at the last stroke of midnight on the last day of every year on every continent. The poetry of Robert Burns, both in Scots and English, has become an important part of Scottish national identity. His personality, democratic and generous, has also become an ideal for many Scots.

The photographers Ross Gillespie and Tricia Malley have marked the Homecoming celebration by making a series of portraits of prominent Scots and adopted Scots. Each sitter has been asked to select and respond to a quotation from Burns, and to reflect upon the continued relevance of Burns in modern Scotland.

The resulting portraits and commentaries, brought together in this book, make for a celebration of contemporary Scottish culture, and a reinforcement of the values and aspirations that found their perfect expression in the poetry of Robert Burns.

Of the numerous would-be portraits of Robert Burns that have come to light over the years since his death, all but six have proved to be cases of wishful thinking, mistaken identity, copies of copies, or deliberate fakery. Only six are accepted as 'authentic' portraits – that is portraits known to have been painted from the life. All six are in the collection of the Scottish National Portrait Gallery. Authenticity in historical portraiture is important, not only because we can be confident about the likeness, but because when we look at such a portrait, we feel that we are looking at the face of a long-dead sitter. It is the business of the portrait to keep the dead, in some sense, alive and present.

The best known portrait of Burns is that painted by his friend Alexander Nasmyth, in 1787. It is instantly recognisable because it has been reproduced so often. As Burns himself remarked, it was as a result of this portrait and the engraving based on it, in the Edinburgh edition of the Poems, that his *'phiz'* had become *'sae kenspeckle'*.

Like all good portraitists, Nasmyth wanted to show more than the appearance of his subject. Ross and Tricia have carried on this tradition capturing not only a physical likeness of their sitters but also something of their essence.

Nasmyth depicted Burns as the young handsome poet – the large shining eyes denoting a man of sensibility. Trees in the background provide a setting for the man of nature; one, as he said of himself, who had *'unbounded good-will to every creature rational or irrational.'* Nasmyth also portrayed his fellow radical. The two men shared republican aspirations and a belief in equality and individual freedom. Portraiture had once been the preserve of the rich, the landed gentry not the tenant farmer. Now – the portrait seems to declare – it is the man himself, not his station in society or his wealth, that counts. *'The rank is but the guinea's stamp; The man's the gowd for a' that.'*

Julie Lawson

Senior Curator, Scottish National Portrait Gallery

Robert Burns by Alexander Nasmyth

As Others See Us

Introduction

Morning; Ayrshire

This is the story of an infant born in a two-roomed cottage which still sits by a roadside in rural western Ayrshire. It is the story of how that infant became the man acclaimed, first by his own people and then by modern critical scholarship, as one of the greatest men of literature ever to emerge in Europe. It is the story of a man who was not only a poet, a song writer and collector, but also a ruthless opponent of hypocrisy and intolerance – and a brave advocate of social and parliamentary reform. It is the story of the young farmer whose writings, first laid before his friends and neighbours, were to become the property and the patrimony of mankind.

In November 1757, The Rev. James MacKnight, M.A., arose in the pulpit of his kirk in Maybole, Ayrshire, and spoke the opening words of a drama – the direct result of which is your reading these words today. For the Rev. James intimated that there was a *Purpose of Marriage* between Agnes Brown, spinster, residing at Maybole and William Burnes, bachelor, residing at Alloway in the parish of Ayr. The marriage was to be happy and was to last for 27 years until they were parted by death – and it was in the family's cottage, on Thursday 25 January 1759, that the midwife delivered Agnes Burns of the first of her seven children.

The child was a boy, he was vigorous and strong and, following the old Scottish tradition, he was named after his paternal grandfather, hence Robert. He was to die 37 years later, probably of chronic rheumatic fever in Dumfries, leaving a desolate widow, six children under the age of ten – and a body of song and poetry which will ever be treasured as one of the jewels in the crown of our literature.

The family left the Alloway cottage when Burns was just 7 years old and the poet grew to maturity on his father's Ayrshire farms of Mount Oliphant and Lochlie. A deeply intelligent boy, with a thirst for literature and a blotting-paper mind, his formal education was intermittent, occurring when he could be spared from work on the family farm. Tutored by his father and by John Murdoch, a teacher at the school which would become Ayr Academy, Burns was bilingual in Scots and English, familiar with the classics of Greece and Rome in translation – and with the prose and poetry both of his homeland and of England.

When William Burnes died of tuberculosis in the spring of 1784, Robert and his brother Gilbert took their widowed mother and their sisters to the farm of Mossgiel which sits on the high road between the village of Mauchline and the town of Kilmarnock. Here we see his eye for the agricultural landscape around him and his resonance with the ebb and surge of the seasons upon his farm. These he describes using his command of the great Scots tongue of our forefathers, replete with its graphic imagery and verbal firepower. But above all, he had the ability to marry breadth of vision with that depth of language which is the genesis of great literature. And the poetry began to come.

This was also the time of the development of his championship of the dignity and the worth of the common man. His poetry sings of the freedoms which must be accorded by society and state in order to preserve that dignity and reflect that worth. He wrote in the great *Epistle to Davie*, his friend David Sillar, a minor poet;

> It's no' in titles nor in rank;
> It's no' in wealth like London bank,
>   To purchase peace and rest...
> Nae treasures, nor pleasures,
>   Could make us happy lang,
> The heart's aye the part, ay
>   That makes us right – or wrang.

Nothing was too small to be beneath his notice. Ploughing for his spring barley in the parks of Mossgiel, he drove the ploughshare, the *coulter*, through the nest of a fieldmouse. He first addresses the mouse in pure Scots;

> Wee, sleekit, cow'rin, tim'rous beastie...

Then switches to pure English to apologise that;

> Man's dominion, has broken Nature's
> social union...

And ends with a final switch from the concrete to the abstract in reflecting that;

> The best laid schemes of mice and men
>   Gang aft a'gley
> And leave us nought but grief an' pain,
>   For promised Joy...

This masterly handling of both languages has an intimacy born of the fact that his poems are not simply descriptive – but autobiographical. It's his interaction with his fellow creatures that arrests our attention – including even a *pediculus capitis* (the common head louse) which, as it marched across a lady's bonnet in church, triggered one of his most celebrated lines;

> O wad some pow'r the Giftie gie us
>   To see ourselves as others see us
> It wad frae mony a blunder free us
>   And foolish notion...

Such foolish notions included, Burns believed, those of the orthodox Calvinist wing of the Kirk, and he trained his verse artillery on certain elements of the Kirk in Mauchline. Taking careful aim, he opened fire on William 'Holy Willie' Fisher, of the neighbouring farm of Montgarswood, in what is probably the greatest example of poetical assassination in the language.

> But Lord, remember me and mine
> Wi' mercies temporal and divine!
> That I for grace and gear may shine,
>   Excelled by nane!
> And all the glory shall be Thine!
> Amen! Amen!

The Kirk however was not without its own spiritual weaponry and Burns, being Burns, was not slow at furnishing ammunition for the counterattack. Jean Armour, daughter of a Mauchline master mason, was pregnant. Her father, a pillar of the Kirk, was not aware of the liaison between his daughter and Burns whom he regarded as an irreligious freethinking rake. Told of his daughter's condition, James Armour fainted clean away. He was revived with a 'stiff cordial' and got up demanding to know the name of the father. He was told – and down he went again.

The poet, after consideration of his position, decided it might be better to create a new life in the West Indies, but was halted in his preparations by the roar of applause which greeted the

Kilmarnock publication in July 1786 of *Poems, chiefly in the Scottish dialect.*

He was strongly advised against emigration by his neighbour Prof. Dugald Stewart who held the chair of moral philosophy at the University of Edinburgh. He was told that his way ahead lay not Westward to Jamaica, but Eastward...

High Noon; Edinburgh

In the Capital he was lionised. He was the star of the social season in the winter of 1786-1787, introduced to high society by his three Ayrshire patrons, Prof. Dugald Stewart; James, Earl of Glencairn and the Lord Provost, Sir James Hunter Blair. There were society breakfasts, literary lunches, evening receptions, dinners and balls. He was hailed at a Masonic gathering as *'Caledonia's Bard'* and kissed the unmarked grave of his mentor Robert Fergusson in the Canongate kirkyard, over whom he erected a handsome inscribed stone. Alison Cockburn, author of *'The Flowers of the Forest'* wrote to a friend; *'The town is agog with the ploughman poet...'* And Prof. Stewart remarked that the adulation he received *'...would have turned any head but his own.'*

It did not turn his head and, sharing a lodging in the Old Town with his Ayrshire friend John Richmond, he set about producing an enlarged and improved second edition of his poems. Glencairn introduced him to William Creech who would become his publisher, the poems being printed by William Smellie, founder and first editor of the

Encyclopaedia Britannica and who was to become a bosom friend. Smellie had also founded that great convivial dining club the Crochallan Fencibles which met in Dawney Douglas's Tavern in the Anchor Close. Here Burns could escape the conventions of high society into the Fencibles rumbustious all-male company.

Creech brought out the Edinburgh edition in the spring of 1787, just after Burns and the teenage Walter Scott had had their celebrated encounter as guests of Prof. Adam Ferguson in the presence of some of the brightest stars of the Enlightenment including the economist Adam Smith.

Already his poetry was largely behind him and, although he continued to write verse for the rest of his life, his principal function henceforward was to be song collecting and song writing. He had been invited by James Johnson, another Fencible, to collaborate in the collection and publication of the large – and largely neglected – corpus of Scottish vernacular folksong. Johnson was about to bring out the first of six volumes of *The Scots Musical Museum* of which Burns was to become literary editor in all but name. And so, in May 1787, armed with the proceeds of his Edinburgh edition the poet turned songwriter embarked upon the second phase of his literary life.

Afternoon; Scotland

Burns undertook three song-collecting tours in the spring summer and autumn of 1787; first to the Borders and indeed over the Border briefly, with Robert Ainslie, a young lawyer friend from Edinburgh;

then to the West Highlands alone and finally there came the great northern tour. Here he travelled in style in a carriage with William Nicol, Classics Master of the High School of Edinburgh, a hard drinking, irascible and brilliant classical scholar. *'Travelling with Nicol'*, Burns wrote wearily, *'was like travelling with a loaded Blunderbuss at half-cock'*. Off they set across West Lothian, up through Stirlingshire, Perthshire to Inverness-shire and then back down through Aberdeen, the Mearns, Angus and finally home to Edinburgh after a round trip of over 500 miles.

Throughout these tours the poet took down, from the singing of the men and women, from fishwives and farmers' wives and from men of all conditions and backgrounds, the folk songs of his country.

This was a tradition which was in danger of being lost for want of being transcribed, set to music and published. From then to the end of his life he saw published through his Edinburgh collaborators, James Johnson and George Thomson, some 400 of our songs in Johnson's *Scots Musical Museum* and in Thomson's *Select Scottish Airs*. All human life is in these songs; songs of farming, songs of fighting, songs of meeting, songs of loving, songs of parting. And just as the portraits of the great Raeburn captured the faces of that remarkable generation of Enlightenment Scotland so Burns captured their music, their songs, their aspirations – and their history.

Of all the songs, the most famous are the love songs, their artistry capturing all the passion, all the pain and, in just a few lines, penetrating to the innermost labyrinth of the human heart.

Lovers meeting;

Yestreen when to the trembling string
    The dance gae'd through the lichted ha'
To thee my fancy took its wing,
    I looked but neither heard nor saw...

Mary Morison

And loving;

So fair art thou, my bonie lass
    So deep in luve am I;
And I will love thee still, my Dear,
    Till a' the seas gang dry...

A red, red Rose

And parting;

Had we never lov'd sae kindly,
    Had we never lov'd sae blindly !
Never met – or never parted,
    We had ne'er been broken-hearted –

Ae fond Kiss

These, and literally scores of other songs, he brought back to Edinburgh, some in fragmentary form, some fully finished. He lived and worked during the winter of 1787–88 in the St James's Square home of his great friend William Cruickshank, a master at the High School. The daughter of the house, Jenny Cruickshank, aged 12, a beautiful and musically gifted child, would play a chosen air over and over on the harpsichord, as the poet sat beside her at a table strewn with a mass of papers – drafting and redrafting and crafting the words until they fitted the air like a lady's hand in a silken glove.

To Jenny he presented an inscribed Edinburgh edition of his Poems and dedicated one of his most beautiful songs to *'My great friend – a very young Lady'*. For the poet always paid his dues. No man or woman either, ever did him a favour and lived to regret the day. The song he dedicated to her was, appropriately,
The Rosebud:

> A rosebud by my early walk
> adown a corn enclosed bawk
> sae gently bent its thorny stalk
> all on a dewy morning.

The greatest of the historically based songs is, of course, the song which Burns put into the mouth of our hero King. It deals with that midsummer morning, nearly seven hundred years ago upon the Carse of Stirling, when on the day that our forefathers swore that they would be masters of the field – or lie beneath it forever.

> But wha, for Scotland's King and Law,
> Freedom's sword will strongly draw,
> Free men stand – and free men fa'
> Let him –*follow me!*
> Robert Bruce's March

In these four superb lines Burns manages to capture the animal magnetism, the oratory, the sheer quality of leadership of the King.

They did indeed follow him and, as was to be said centuries later, they fought like Scotsmen – and they won their freedom.

Evening; Dumfries-shire

But the poet could not tour the country and collect songs for a living. He had to return to work – and he took a farm.

He took Ellisland in Nithsdale, seven miles north of Dumfries. His tenancy of the farm lasted but three years – for although the riverside scenery was outstanding, it was stony ground. Indeed, the poet wrote to a friend that a verse was missing from the Book of Genesis... *'And the Lord riddled all creation – and the riddlings he threw on Ellisland!'* Here Burns began his career as an Excise Officer – and also made the contact which was to produce his most famous narrative poem. At the home of his neighbour and friend Robert Riddell of Glenriddell, he was introduced to the famous English antiquary Francis Grose, who came originally from Surrey.

Grose, going to Ayrshire to collect materials for a forthcoming book on historical sites, asked Burns what might be included. The poet suggested the ghost-haunted Kirk of Alloway, hard by his own birthplace. This was accepted by Grose on one condition – that Burns supplied him with a poem describing one of the witches' Sabbaths said to be held there on stormy nights. And that is how the splendid *Tam O' Shanter* rode out into literary history from the pages of Volume II of *Grose's Antiquities of Scotland*.

In 1791 Robert and Jean Burns moved their young family to Dumfries where his last five years were to be spent. Misfortune began to crowd in upon him at this time. His health began materially to fail. He was subject to repeated attacks of what was probably chronic rheumatic fever, a disease for which there was then no treatment. In 1791 came the early death of his friend and patron the Earl of Glencairn, head of the old Ayrshire family of the

Cunninghams – and the subject of the great *Lament for James, Earl of Glencairn* with its powerful concluding stanza:

> The mother may forget the child
> That smiles so sweetly at her knee –
> But I'll remember you, Glencairn
> – and all that thou has done for me.

He was also in trouble for the radical political opinions which he never cared to hide. The poet was not a revolutionary but he was a radical and a reformer. But these were dangerous views in the Britain of 1792 where the government of William Pitt was extremely edgy in the aftermath of the loss of our American Colonies and in the light of the French Revolution now in full swing across the Channel.

Burns was carpeted by his Excise superiors and formally reminded that he was a civil servant, a government officer and was warned that he was paid to act, not think. He was told in effect: *Burns, watch your tongue – and watch your pen. For you yourself are being watched...* But by this time he had begun to die – and death came for him slowly. Chronic rheumatic fever was the diagnosis first advanced by the physician Sir James Crichton-Brown and is generally agreed today.

His own physician, Dr. Maxwell, sent him to the sea-bathing station at Brow Well on the Solway. He knew that death was close, for it is near Brow that the great river Nith, having flowed past his old farm of Ellisland and then past his house in Dumfries town, finally reaches the Solway – and its journey's end. He came home to die, nursed by Jean and their young neighbour Jessie Lewars, for whom he wrote the last of his songs *'O wert thou in the cauld blast, on yonder lea...'* The merciful release finally came on 21 July 1796.

Four days later, to the strains of Handel's 'Dead March' from *Saul*, his coffin was taken on a gun carriage from the Town House of Dumfries before thousands of silent mourners. Jean Armour was not among them. She was in labour with her last child, Maxwell, who was being born even as his father was being borne to his burying in St Michael's Kirkyard.

The crowds dispersed and there then followed the short summer night. The day after the funeral was a glorious cloudless day of High Summer and as Hans Hecht reflected in his great biography of Robert Burns; *'the Sun, which rose so early on the Morrow over the sleeping town and cast his beams on the fresh earth of the new grave – that was surely the Sun of Immortality...'*

Professor David W Purdie

Janice Galloway
Novelist

I'm from Ayrshire, so Burns has always loomed large – school competitions and the like did not put me off. I sang *'Ca' the Yowes'* at Burns suppers as a teenager, sometimes as the only woman present, and loved the eerie quiet of the words before I really knew what it meant.

Songs to country girls are a stock in trade in folk song circles, but Burns' are special. That she is *'fair and lovely'* is an unlikely thing, given the arduousness of minding yowes – out in all weathers from the age of ten, sleeping on the hillside, zero to meagre pay – but Burns imagines her as heroic, calling the sheep to the swollen waters of the burn in the evening to keep them safe, being his *'Bonnie Dearie'*. And the melody, an almost modal minor tune, is completely haunting.

Sing it yourself, unaccompanied – it's the only way.

Ca' the Yowes to the Knowes

Ca' the yowes to the knowes
Ca' them whare the heather grows
Ca' then whare the burnie rowes,
My bonnie Dearie.

As I gaed down the water-side,
There I met my Shepherd-lad:
He row'd me sweetly in his plaid,
And he ca'd me his Dearie.

Edwin Morgan
Scotland's National Poet

This poem offers a very interesting, unusual slant on the Highland Clearances, as it deals with early attempts to prevent the Highlanders from emigrating to the New World. It made a strong impression on me as a poem, but it is particularly interesting that someone renowned as a lyric poet should also write such a powerful satirical work. It almost needs a key and notes to get the full meaning from it. Some commentators did not like this contrast with Burns's lyricism, but it is all to the good that a poet can write both satirical and love poetry.

Burns is the great example of a thinking man, gradually learning how many things he could do well, looking round the society of his own time and responding to it in his poetry. Here he mentions both his contemporaries, such as George Washington, and historical figures from the past that match the unscrupulous landowners of his day, and who are promised a similar reward in hell. This range of reference is all to the good. At the time, it was unusual to possess such a poetic range, but in Shakespeare's and Milton's time it was accepted that a poet should cast his mind widely. Burns had a sharp eye, a sharp ear, a sharp tongue – and enjoyed riling his contemporaries. It was excellent that he was able to do this as skillfully and energetically as he does here.

The Address of Beelzebub (The Devil) to;
The Rt. Hon. John, Earl of Breadalbane;
1786 A.D (5790 A.M)

Go on, my Lord! I lang to meet you
An' in my HOUSE AT HAME to greet you:
Wi' COMMON LORDS ye shanna mingle
The benmost newk, beside the ingle
At my right hand, assign'd your seat
'Tween HEROD's hip and POLYCRATE
A seat, I'm sure ye're weel deservin't;
  An' till ye come – your humble servant,
       BEELZEBUB

HELL, 1st June, *Anno Mundi* 5790.

Patrick Doyle
Composer

I was brought up with and still am surrounded by terrific singers in my life and their staple diet was songs by Robert Burns, which I ate up. My grandmother, who had a lovely soprano voice, is encyclopaedic about Burns and quotes him endlessly. Through her love and knowledge of his songs, my mother and father to this day constantly sing and quote the Bard to highlight the machinations of human nature.

Naturally I now do the same thing. It's a joy that this great man's philosophies are quoted all over the world.

'O wad some Power the giftie gie us,
To see oursels as ithers see us!'

I heard these lines many times growing up. I remember what a thrill it was when I first read this poem in Primary School and immediately recognised these two lines as words of wisdom plagiarised by my parents.

This poem is one of the great levellers. I love the *'fur coat and nae knickers'* aspect of it.

The imagery is so filmic; the close up of the wig and bonnet to catch a glimpse of the indiscriminate louse. I hear the music right now; light-hearted mixed with liturgical.

As a child I loved the image of this grand, authoritarian Lady being brought down to earth, without knowing it. It was our little secret and Burns immediately fills the reader with quiet smugness and a satisfying belief that no one is better than anyone else.

The imagery of this work is both empowering and inspirational and is a salutary lesson to us all.

To a Louse

O wad some Pow'r the giftie gie us
To see oursels as others see us!
It wad frae monie a blunder free us
    An' foolish notion:
What airs in dress an' gait wad lea'e us,
    And ev'n Devotion!

Eddi Reader
Musician, singer and songwriter

While making an album of Robert Burns' music
and words, I travelled millions of miles in his company.
I searched gravestones for his friends and his
companions; I stood in the rain outside doorways
he had stood in; I drank in bars he had drunk in;
I marvelled at the beauty he saw from the hills
of Galloway and the Heads of Ayr and I am convinced
that I was directed by him in my choices for the album.
The book of his work that I was collecting from
continually opened, Harry Potter-like, at the page
that contained the words of the poem *'Willie Stewart'*
until the day it magically fell open at a poem called
'Polly Stewart'. Polly was Willie's daughter and I decided
to insert it into my version of Willie Stewart. After getting
loads of praise for my album, I went back to Dumfries
to visit Burns' last home and found the lines to half the
verses engraved on a back window in a hidden room.
I felt his company once more.

Thank you, Robert. I love you x

Lovely Polly Stewart

The flower it blaws, it fades, it fa's,
And art can ne'er renew it;
But Worth and Truth eternal youth
Will gie to Polly Stewart.

May he whase arms shall fauld thy charms,
Possess a leal and true heart!
To him be given, to ken the Heaven
He holds in Polly Stewart!

Neil Gillon
Ayrshire farmer

I suppose it is being on the land myself and Burns being a man of the land that makes this poem stick with me. He was so connected with the land and I think that is something we have lost today.

Nowadays it is all about big tractors and 20 tonne machinery that costs thousands of pounds. In the past sheep farmers used to walk the hills. They heard the birds and watched the land under their feet changing. We don't have that everyday contact with the land anymore. Maybe that's where we are going wrong.

When Burns wrote, *'I'm truly sorry Man's dominion, Has broken Nature's social union,'* well, we are still doing that today. But here's a man who wrote that over 200 years ago before anyone was thinking about conservation or the environment. He was just a man doing a job and writing what he saw. But he was also asking us to look for ourselves.

To A Mouse, On turning her up in her Nest, with the Plough

Still, thou art blest, compar'd wi' *me*!
The *present* only toucheth thee:
But Och! I *backward* cast my e'e.
On prospects drear!
An' *forward*, tho' I canna see,
I *guess* an' fear!

Christopher Brookmyre
Novelist

'*Tam O' Shanter*' makes a riotous cautionary tale out of an uncomfortable national truth, pitting its vainglorious '*everybam*' figure against demons both of the imagination and of the inner self.

Scotland has a brutal, bloody and embarrassing history of supernatural credulity. The nation of David Hume and James Clerk Maxwell is also the country of James VI and his *Daemonologie*, of witch-burning and religious hysteria.

More pertinently, it also has a brutal, bloody and embarrassingly on-going history of alcohol abuse. '*Wi usquabae, we'll face the devil!*' The 'water of life' renders us fearless enough to fight the most monstrous of foes, but more often renders us insensible enough to imagine monstrous foes where none exist, then disastrously to fight any proxy who happens along at the wrong time. Thus we can sympathise with Tam but never admire him, for any heroics he performs are purely to extricate himself from the kind of situation you might get yourself into '*whene'er to drink you are inclin'd*'.

Tam O' Shanter

Whiles holding fast his gude blue bonnet;
Whiles crooning o'er some auld Scots sonnet;
Whiles glow'rin round wi' prudent cares,
Lest bogles catch him unawares:
Kirk-Alloway was drawing nigh,
Where ghaists and houlets nightly cry.

　　Inspiring bold *John Barleycorn!*
What dangers thou canst make us scorn!
Wi' tippeny, we fear nae evil;
Wi' usquabae, we'll face the devil!

Alex Fergusson MSP
Presiding Officer of the Scottish Parliament

As a sheep farmer of some 30 years experience, I can verify there is nothing more *'unco mournfu'* than coming upon a *'cowpie'* – a sheep stuck on its back in a hollow or ditch – a situation that will invariably lead to its death through suffocation unless it is righted timeously. The risk is greater when the sheep is in full fleece and, if death results, the shepherd will have motherless lambs to rear.

This was the gruesome fate that befell poor Mailie, grazing only within the confines that her tether would allow. And that tether proved her downfall, literally, as she tripped over it one day and stumbled into a ditch, falling fatally onto her back. Hughoc, a neighbouring farm labourer, happened upon her, and the poem relates the words that Mailie spoke to him with her dying breaths.

Of both her offspring she entreated:

'And may they never learn the gaets,
Of ither vile, wanrestfu' Pets!

And she gave them a strict moral lecture, pleading to her son:

'An' warn him, what I winna name,
To stay content wi yowes, at hame.'

The poem's words contain so much more than a final entreaty to ensure that her offspring are raised properly. They contain a vision for the enlightenment of man, for the benefits of a loving home and of living a lawful life and a warning against giving in to temptations, all of which we hear echoed today. Finally, Mailie pleads of her offspring:

'An' when ye think upon your Mither,
Mind to be kind to ane anither.'

If you add in tongue, or country, or even earth after the word 'Mither', you'll see what I mean.

It's about standards, it's about success, security and sense of worth and decency. It's pure Burnsian brilliance and it's absolute magic.

The Death and Dying Words of Poor Mailie, the Author's Only Pet Yowe, an Unco' Mournfu' Tale

'And now, *my bairns,* wi' my last breath,
I lea'e my blessin wi' you baith:
An' when ye think upo' your Mither,
Mind to be kind to ane anither'

Hardeep Singh Kohli
Author and Broadcaster

Some people write Burns off as merely a romantic poet and a songsmith but work like *'Such a Parcel of Rogues in a Nation'* shows Burns to be passionately political when it comes to the constitutional future of the Scottish nation. Scotland and the Scots seem to historically blame the English for everything. Burns manages to rise above such petty politics to see the whole issue in context. He blames the Scots for selling their ain folk out; and the price was paid in English gold. This searing political insight was some two hundred years ahead of its time. Scotland's destiny rests in Scotland's hands.

Such a Parcel of Rogues in a Nation

Fareweel to a' our Scottish fame,
 Fareweel our ancient glory;
Fareweel even to the Scottish name,
 Sae fam'd in martial story!
Now Sark rins o'er the Solway sands,
 And Tweed rins to the ocean,
To mark whare England's province stands,
 Such a parcel of rogues in a nation!

Peter Capaldi
Actor

Is it because he was an awesome philanderer, or despite it, that Burns' understanding of love seems so acute? When he writes, as he often does, of melancholic partings, or the bittersweet victory of love in the battle against age and fate, he rises above the sentimental and presents us with a truth recognisable to everyone who knows what love is.

My Jean – a Fragment

Though Cruel Fate should bid us part
 Far as the pole and line
Her dear idea round my heart
 Should tenderly entwine.

Though mountains rise, and deserts howl,
 And oceans roar between;
Yet dearer than my deathless soul
 I still would love my Jean.

Aamer Anwar
Human rights lawyer

Burns was a poet of the common man who championed universal suffrage and the abolition of slavery long before it became fashionable. Inspired by the American and French Revolutions with their ideas of liberty, equality and fraternity, Burns stood against the corruption of the gentry, nobility and royalty.

The Victorian upper classes tried to sanitise the radical Burns into a tartan shortbread icon with drunken suppers in the name of culture, but the real Robert Burns wrote about poverty and the injustice of the class system, and wanted to make the world a better place.

His songs and satire still enrich that struggle against oppression and injustice and I believe we owe it to Robert Burns to explain who he really was and what he stood for.

For me, *'The Tree of Liberty'*, written in support of the ideals of the French Revolution provides that explanation.

The Tree of Liberty

Wi' plenty o' sic trees, I trow,
The warld would live in peace, man;
The sword would help to mak a plough,
The din o' war wad cease, man.
Like brethren in a common cause,
We'd on each other smile, man;
And equal rights and equal laws,
Wad gladden every isle, man.

Wae worth the loon wha wadna eat
Sic halesome dainty cheer, man;
I'd gie my shoon frae aff my feet,
To taste sic fruit, I swear, man.

Rt Hon Alex Salmond MP MSP
First Minister of Scotland

If I had to choose my favourite Scot of all time I would choose Robert Burns. Our national bard has established himself as Scotland's greatest cultural icon and the nation's favourite son.

The poetry of Robert Burns has carried Scots to an audience beyond our shores and adds real colour to the Scottish tartan. Burns forms a substantial part of the articulation of Scottish identity. His work contained virtues that have been absorbed into our sense of self – it is humorous, radical and articulate.

If I had to choose from his canon of work I would select *'A Man's a Man for a' That'* as my favourite Burns poem. His body of work has stood the test of time and continues to influence and inspire people across the world.

For a' that and a' that

Then let us pray that come it may,
    As come it will for a' that,
That Sense and Worth, o'er a' the earth
    Shall bear the gree, and a' that.
  For a' that, and a' that,
    It's comin yet for a' that
That Man to Man the warld o'er,
    Shall brothers be for a' that.

Jim McColl
Entrepreneur, Clyde Blowers

My whole career I've come across people jostling for position within an organisation, some of whom are just full of their own self importance and don't have the ability to see themselves as others see them. But if they did it would make them a much better leader, and person.

It is something I often think about in my approach to building businesses. We have to listen to each other. So we try to build a more inclusive team approach where everybody gets to say what they think, even if it is not what others want to hear.

However, it is also a Scottish trait to often think that other people know more and know better than us. But I've found that whenever I've travelled abroad for business they often see us as better than we see ourselves. That's the other side of what the poem is all about, it is telling you to step back a bit, think about what others see and recognise the good in yourself as well.

To a Louse

O wad some Pow'r the giftie gie us
To see oursels as others see us!
It wad frae monie a blunder free us
    An' foolish notion:
What airs in dress an' gait wad lea'e us,
    And ev'n Devotion!

Denise Mina
Novelist

This sums up so many things about Burns that I love and find forgotten: he's a messy hero, the best and tastiest kind. He wrote poems with the 'c' word in them, was a cheeky bugger, pass-remarkable, occasionally snide and sometimes bitter. Almost anyone who reads a lot of his work will find something in it to offend them, and challenging is exactly what ferocious honesty should do.

This scrap of a poem is a painful reminder that no matter how much artists hope to capture angels, most of us are really documenting our devils and then charging the public to peer at them.

For me the truly great thing about Burns is his accessibility. There's no glory in making a reader feel they'd be able to see your soul if only they'd done a degree or read the classics. Burns is as comprehensible as an advert.

There's an epigram in a synagogue in Prague which is so beautiful that I've copied it into every notebook I've had since. Written of a man long dead, it is a glorious claim that could be said of few but can be truly said of Burns:

'Here lies a man who understood the beauty of songs.'

Epigram to a Painter

Dear --, I'll gie ye some advice
    You'll tak it no uncivil:
You shoudna paint at angels man
    But try and paint the Devil.

To paint an angel's kittle wark,
    Wi' Nick there's little danger;
You'll easy draw a lang-kent face,
    But no sae weel a stranger.

Sir Moir Lockhead
Entrepreneur, FirstGroup Plc

We have lived in Scotland almost as long as we've
lived anywhere. We came here in 1979, nearly 30
years ago, so half our lives so far. It was very easy
to move here. It is a very straightforward place
to live and work – a great place to do business.
Scots make you feel part of the community very quickly.
It's pretty easy to fit in. Now we both absolutely look
at this as home. And as our family grows so too does
our connection with Scotland. All our grandchildren
are Scottish. We are very lucky that we have all stayed
close and live within 20 miles of each other.

I picked *'My love is like a red red rose'* because
it's my wife's favourite and it just sums everything up.
Hopefully that will keep me in the good books!

A red, red Rose

O my Luve's like a red, red rose,
    That's newly sprung in June;
O my Luve's like the melodie
    That's sweetly play'd in tune --

Sir Malcolm MacGregor
of MacGregor
Clan chief

The words I have chosen from Robert Burns sums up what I hope people feel when they journey not only to the Highlands but to Scotland in general. That whenever they visit there is a Highland welcome in store, in the finest tradition of Highland hospitality.

This is part of the ambience of being in Scotland. Warm and friendly greetings have always been part of our culture which comes, in part, from our clannish identity and idea of community spirit.

Over the years many people have ventured to Scotland in search of their roots or simply to soak up the atmosphere of dramatic glens, glistening mountain tops, wild rivers, beautiful gardens, remote graveyards and old castles from a more distant period. The idea of a Highland welcome reflects that feeling of affinity and connectedness, which exists between Scots wherever they may be in the world.

The clan system such as it is, is a worldwide phenomenon, unique to Scotland, being based on mutual kinship and a shared history. For those who make the long journey to their homeland, there will always be that special Highland welcome, which so invigorated the great bard himself when he was on the road all those years ago.

The Highland Welcome

When death's dark stream I ferry o'er
A time that surely shall come;
In Heaven itself I'll ask no more,
Than just a Highland welcome.

Liz Lochhead
Poet and playwright

What do I like about Mary Morison?
Especially my chosen second stanza?

Well, the words really, simple as that.
(I'd like to think in all this *'The Homecoming'* hoo-ha
somewhere there'll be people going: Listen to this
then just saying the words out loud, exactly as
Burns wrote them.)

Is this 'my favourite bit of Burns'? No. I have hundreds
of these, been storing them up in my living imagination –
and, I regret to admit, my cache of cliches – ever since
I was a wean from a Lanarkshire primary school reciting
at the Miners' Welfare Two Hundredth Anniversary Verse
Speaking Competition and Burns became (for good
and ill) to me the very image and archetype of The Bard.

In this verse of this song we get: a close up of a bow
on the strings of a fiddle; cut to a wide-shot then
pan-through that dance in the lighted ha'; then –
via 'this', 'that', 'yon' – a celebration of the specific
and the particular. Of Mary Morison...

Mary Morison

Yestreen when to the trembling string
  The dance gaed through the lighted ha',
To thee my fancy took its wing,
  I sat, but neither heard, nor saw:
Though this was fair, and that was braw,
  And yon the toast of a' the town,
I sigh'd and said amang them a',
  'Ye are na Mary Morison'

Peter Howson
Artist

Burns was a romantic and I'm a romantic, not in that sickly sweet Mills and Boon fashion but romantic in the sense that we will always oppose the classicists and we will always question the establishment.

Burns intoxicated me; his legendary life of womanising, love making, drinking and debauchery just enthralled me. This was a man that could write such beautiful poems and yet could be so flawed and had endured such tragedy. I guess I recognised a kindred spirit in him; a tortured soul. He was simply a genius and this poem in particular is a work of genius.

It is satirical, funny, pokes fun at the establishment and is completely timeless – it could have been written today. Burns wasn't not a believer so he was not poking fun at God but he was poking fun at people's perceptions of God and at the hypocrisy that can exist within the church. I am also a Christian and I have fought bigotry all my life and what this poem did at the time was change perceptions and that is a remarkable thing.

Burns was a rebel and he made people think. That's what art is all about for me; making people question and open doors into another world. Burns ignited my spark and that's all I can ever hope to do to others.

Holy Willie's Prayer

Yet I am here, a chosen sample,
To shew Thy grace is great and ample:
I'm here, a pillar o' Thy temple
    Strong as a rock,
A guide, a ruler and example
    To a' Thy flock. –

Professor Sir Ian Wilmut
Scientist

'For a' that, and a' that,
It's comin yet for a' that,
That Man to Man the warld o'er,
Shall brothers be for a' that.'

Although this and several other declarations of human rights were written at the end of the 18th century, it was not until 1946 that the World Health Organisation was the first to assert that *'enjoyment of the highest attainable standard of health'* is a human right. One measure of the standard of health of a community is average lifespan, although this is influenced by many social factors. This is now around 80 years in richer countries but in poorer parts of the world it is less than 40 years. Even in these poorer places it would be comparatively easy to prevent the death of thousands of children each day from illness that could be treated or avoided. Within our own country it is shocking to see a difference of 28 years between two neighbouring communities in Glasgow (Calton and Lenzie).

A change of priorities in biomedical research could benefit poorer communities. At present 90% of this research is concerned with afflictions of the 10% of the population who live in richer areas. Should we place greater emphasis on developing treatments that are important everywhere and can be administered anywhere?

For a' that and a' that

Then let us pray that come it may,
    As come it will for a' that,
That Sense and Worth, o'er a' the earth
    Shall bear the gree, and a' that.
    For a' that, and a' that,
        It's comin yet for a' that
That Man to Man the warld o'er,
    Shall brothers be for a' that.

Professor Janice Kirkpatrick
Designer, curator and writer

54

What Burns means to me.

Growing up in Dumfries. My Father's middle name.
Burns Mineral Water Works, Peter Burns the town
herbalist, Burns house, Burns Street, Burns statue,
The Auld Brig museum, Burns Mausoleum,
St Michael's Kirkyard, the Black Death, plague graves
and grave robbers.

Burns commemorative stamps in 1966. Laurieknowe
Primary School and Burns by heart. Southwestern speak.
Ca' The Yowes, My Love Is Like A Red, Red, Rose,
To A Mouse, To A Louse. The Observatory, the murderer's
clogs, the drowned man's skull, Sawney Bean and
Tam O' Shanter. Bogles.

Ellisland Farm. Shooting pigeons in winter stubble
near Auldgirth. Fishing the Cluden Water, Nith and Solway.
Sleeket, cowran, tim'rous beasties.

Pints and McKerrows in The Globe. *Guid Nychburris*
and riding his countryside. *The Deil's Awa' Wi'*
Th' Exciseman among Georgian streets and soft red stone.

Leaving for Glasgow. The Trongate and Gallowgate.
The Griffin and the Sarrie Heid. The Merchant City and
Graven Images. Timorous Beasties' Burns Suppers.
Rovin' Scottish mafia in far-flung places. Haggis in
Wellington, Hong Kong and Helsinki.

Then moving to Ayrshire. Burns Cottage, Souter Johnnie's,
thatched roofs, Cassillis and Culzean. NVA at Alloway.
Farming and ploo horses. The dirty hole called Minibole.
Mauchline and Tarbolton. Sweet Afton and the Banks
O' Doon. The Bachelors' Club and The Jolly Beggars.
Burns country, cookery, smokery and B&B. Burns sausage
supper, Hogmanay and whisky. Our immortal memory.
Auld Lang Syne.

Tam O' Shanter

Now, do thy speedy utmost, Meg,
And win the key-stane o' the brig;
There at them thou thy tail may toss,
A running stream they dare na cross.
But ere the keystane she could make,
The fient a tail she had to shake!
For Nannie, far before the rest,
Hard upon noble Maggie prest,
And flew at *Tam* wi' furious ettle;
But little wist she Maggie's mettle –
Ae spring brought off her master hale
Bur left behind her ain grey tail:
The carlin claught her by the rump,
And left poor Maggie scarce a stump.

Andrew O'Hagan
Novelist

No other poet has Burns' gift for camaraderie. To him, fellowship was a religion, and through his poetry we get to feel that empathy is the greatest triumph of human nature.

When I first discovered *'A Man's a Man for a' That'*, I felt like I'd run into a secular hymn to the dignity of the common man that outstrips any holy writ or any national anthem. It is a song for every colour, every class and every creed, to the notion of brotherhood and equality as the greatest testament to humanity's essential compassion, a goal everybody can share.

I always want to post the poem to world leaders whenever they face a crisis: it denotes the creative part played by the human imagination in leaving the world in better shape than we found it. Here was a poor man, a flawed man, doused in adversity, who nevertheless managed to write with beautiful optimism about the future.

'It's comin yet for a' that,' he wrote, *'That Man to Man the warld o'er/Shall brothers be for a' that.'* It was no government, no committee of elders, no faction either, that could write this anthem to the human spirit. Only Burns, a true master of the believing heart.

For a' that and a' that

Then let us pray that come it may,
    As come it will for a' that,
That Sense and Worth, o'er a' the earth
    Shall bear the gree, and a' that.
    For a' that, and a' that,
        It's comin yet for a' that
    That Man to Man the warld o'er,
        Shall brothers be for a' that.

Janice Galloway
Novelist

Location:
Palacerigg Country Park
north east of Glasgow

Christopher Brookmyre
Novelist

Location:
Bothwell Parish Church

Edwin Morgan
Scotland's National Poet

Location:
Glasgow

Alex Fergusson MSP
*Presiding Officer of the
Scottish Parliament*

Location:
The Scottish Parliament
Debating Chamber

Patrick Doyle
Composer

Location:
Sound stage in
Shepperton Studios, England

Hardeep Singh Kohli
Author and broadcaster

Location:
River Tweed at Coldstream

Eddi Reader
*Musician, singer
and songwriter*

Location:
Glasgow

Peter Capaldi
Actor

Location:
Soho, London

Neil Gillon
Ayrshire farmer

Location:
Outbuildings on Neil's farm
near Girvan, Ayrshire

Aamer Anwar
Human rights lawyer

Location:
Glasgow Botanic Gardens

Rt Hon Alex Salmond MP MSP
First Minister of Scotland

Location:
The Scottish Parliament

Liz Lochhead
Poet and playwright

Location:
Department of Scottish Literature,
University of Glasgow

59

Jim McColl
Entrepreneur, Clyde Blowers

Location:
Clyde Blowers head office,
East Kilbride

Peter Howson
Artist

Location:
The artist's studio in Glasgow

Denise Mina
Novelist

Location:
Kelvingrove Art Gallery and
Museum, Glasgow

Professor Sir Ian Wilmut
Scientist

Location:
Chancellors Building,
Little France, Edinburgh

Sir Moir Lockhead
Entrepreneur, FirstGroup Plc

Location:
FirstGroup Plc head office,
Aberdeen

Professor Janice Kirkpatrick
Designer, curator and writer

Location:
On Janice's smallholding in
Ayrshire with her horse Joe

Sir Malcolm MacGregor of MacGregor
Clan chief

Location:
At home in Angus

Andrew O'Hagan
Novelist

Location:
Irvine beach

Reflections

'Making it a reality with Roy and Fiona; listening to Eddi Reader singing along to Van Morrison; chasing sheep around Janice Galloway; laughing till it hurt with Patrick Doyle; snow at Clyde Blowers; lunch with David and Walter; almost getting blown away on Irvine beach with Andrew O'Hagan; meeting Moir again; Denise Mina's painted toenails, all having a go wearing the big black angel wings; being in the Debating Chamber with the Presiding Officer; visiting Gavin in his eyrie; having tea with Malcolm and Fiona MacGregor; appreciating Joanne's enthusiasm; Tricia squealing on the back of Ross Hunter's quad bike; getting soaked with Janice Kirkpatrick and Joe; listening to Liz Lochhead read aloud; on the farm with Neil Gillon; comparing soup recipes with Hardeep Singh Kohli; getting excited about Alan Ainsley's designs; putting the world to rights with Peter Capaldi over a bottle of wine: David Purdie's eagle eye; drying off Aamer's feet; Peter Howson signing a copy of one of his books with a drawing; Julie's steadying hand; meeting Edwin Morgan; Mandy Rhodes burning the midnight oil; getting spooky with Christopher Brookmyre; being grateful for Ian Wilmut's patience when the lights went nuts; the First Minister, the choir and the Christmas carols.

'Thank you to all of the sitters and others who helped along the way, it has been a privilege and a joy.'

Tricia and Ross

'I am very flattered to be part of Ross Gillespie's and Tricia Malley's AS OTHERS SEE US exhibition. Tricia and Ross are real masters and it is a thrill to see my portrait alongside famous Scots.'

Sir Moir Lockhead

'My experience was that it was really good to see, meet and make new friends (especially you two) have a dram, ca' the crack and listen to some of the best of Scottish talent entertaining us at the Homecoming Burns suppers in the finest Scottish tradition as only we can (I'm getting all patriotic now so I think I'll go and have a dram!!)'

Neil Gillon

'I am delighted to have featured in the exhibition and to have had the opportunity to share my own thoughts on what

Burns means to me and to Scotland. The exhibition has been extremely well received at Holyrood, and I have no doubt that it will stir hearts and minds across our nation as it tours across Scotland throughout the Year of Homecoming, ensuring that Burns' legacy continues to be remembered and celebrated.'

Rt Hon Alex Salmond MP MSP

'The AS OTHERS SEE US project attracted me immediately. The connection with Robert Burns was poignant; I knew he had travelled in the highlands but was not sure where. Nonetheless I could imagine him in drovers inns or in conversations with farmers and maybe marvelling at the highland scenery which would have been very different from his home in Ayrshire. The experience of being part of this project made me investigate Burns further and it was wonderful to be included with such a wide variety of people from Scotland. A unique experience and one that I think would make the bard chuckle!'

Sir Malcolm MacGregor

'It is a real pleasure and honour to take part in this event. My wife and I made our home in Scotland more than 35 years ago. I am particularly pleased to celebrate the birth of Burns because so many of the poems that he wrote are as relevant today as they have ever been. He had a great insight into human nature and society. It is a great shame that there is nobody today who has the same vision, compassion and ability to put these sentiments into words that we can all understand and enjoy.'

Professor Sir Ian Wilmut

'It was great fun to create a fully functioning photographic studio in Lindsayston Burn. I'd no idea how Joe (the one with the 'frosty pow') would react as he'd never been exposed to flash photography, or to a few thousand quids' worth of Hasselblad camera equipment. Getting him into the water was easy, as he likes to do anything awkward and is used to getting his feet washed in the burn. Thankfully he ignored the flash but was very interested in Ross's silver reflector and he did try to eat the camera. He gave me a right good soaking which was a welcome distraction from the trauma of getting my picture taken.'

Professor Janice Kirkpatrick

'This was doubtless the most intriguing photo shoot I have ever sat (or stood) for, albeit one whose results I looked forward to with a degree of trepidation, possibly owing to a childhood incident. When my parents dressed me up for Halloween at the age of three, I took one look at my reflection in a mirror and promptly burst into tears. When my dad asked what was wrong, I replied: "I'm feart of my ain self".'

Christopher Brookmyre

'Thanks to Tricia and Ross for taking my picture. Sitting for a photograph is always difficult for me but they made me feel comfortable and I didn't feel like they had stolen my soul. My picture was taken on the second floor of a place in the centre of town. The window looked out onto Bath Street and I was looking out at all the shoppers going home on the top deck of the bus. While Tricia talked of her bonny cottage up north, I imagined my escape to some scenic heaven.'

Eddi Reader

'I have had many cameras thrust in my face. That is the lot of an international love-god and style icon (which I am). However, I have never experienced such a creative and rewarding shoot as that I had with Ross and Tricia. And they gave me soup. Really nice soup. Homemade soup. I miss them. And the soup.'

Hardeep Singh Kohli

Glossary

a' – all
adown – beside
ae – one
aff – off
ain – own
amang – among
an' – and, if
ane – one
anither – another
awa – away
bairns – children
baith – both
bawk – unploughed land among corn
beasties – diminutive beast
benmost newk – furthest corner
blaws – blows
blunder – mistake
bogles – spirits, hobgoblins
braw – fine, handsome
burnie rowes – small stream flows
ca'd – hammered
Caledonia's Bard – Scotland's Poet
canna – can't
carlin – a witch
cauld – cold
claught – snatched at, laid hold of
cowran – cowering
Deil's – Devil's
e'e – eye
ettle – intent
exciseman – taxman
fa' – fall

fa's – falls
fareweel – farewell
fauld – to fold. A fold for sheep
fient – no i.e. an absence
frae – from
gae'd – went
gaets – ways
gang aft a'gley – go often wrong
ghaists – ghosts
gie – give
gude – good
giftie gie – gift to give
glow'rin – gaze intently
gowd – gold
gree – to agree
ha' – hall
hale – whole
halesome – wholesome
hame – home
houlets – owls
ither – other
kenspeckle – easily recognised
key-stane – keystone
kittle wark – easy work
knowes – a knoll, a small round hill
lang – long
lea'e – leave
leal – loyal, true, faithful
lichted ha' – lighted hall
lang-kent – long known
luve's – love is
mither – mother

mony – many

mournfu' – sorrowful

na – no

nae – no

nane – none

o'er – over

on prospects drear – dreary prospects

oursel's – ourselves

phiz' – the human face

play'd – played

ploo horses – plough horses

Polycrate – Polycrates

Pow'r – Power

prest – pressed

rins – runs, melts

row'd – wrapped

sae – so

sae fam'd – so famous

sae weel – so well

shanna – shall not

shew – show

shoon – shoes

shoudna – should not

sic – such

sigh'd – sighed

sleeket – sleek, smooth

smallholding – a small farm

tak – take

th' – the

tim'rous – timid

tippeny – 'twopenny'
(stong ale with a two pennies tax on it)

toucheth – touches

trow – believe

tween – between

unco mournfu' – very sorrowful

wad – would

wadna – wouldn't

wae – woe

wanrestfu' – restless

warld – world

wert – were

wha – who

whare – where

whase – whose

wi – with

wi' Nick – with the Devil

wi' usquabae – with whisky,
the Water of Life (Gaelic)

winna – will not

wist – anticipated

wrang – wrong

ye – you

ye're weel deservin't – you well deserve it

yestreen – yesterday

yon – that

yowe – ewe

Luath Press Limited

committed to publishing well written books worth reading

LUATH PRESS takes its name from Robert Burns, whose little collie Luath (*Gael.,* swift or nimble) tripped up Jean Armour at a wedding and gave him the chance to speak to the woman who was to be his wife and the abiding love of his life. Burns called one of 'The Twa Dogs' Luath after Cuchullin's hunting dog in Ossian's *Fingal.* Luath Press was established in 1981 in the heart of Burns country, and is now based a few steps up the road from Burns' first lodgings on Edinburgh's Royal Mile.

Luath offers you distinctive writing with a hint of unexpected pleasures.

Most bookshops in the UK, the US, Canada, Australia, New Zealand and parts of Europe either carry our books in stock or can order them for you. To order direct from us, please send a £sterling cheque, postal order, international money order or your credit card details (number, address of cardholder and expiry date) to us at the address below. Please add post and packing as follows: UK – £1.00 per delivery address; overseas surface mail – £2.50 per delivery address; overseas airmail – £3.50 for the first book to each delivery address, plus £1.00 for each additional book by airmail to the same address. If your order is a gift, we will happily enclose your card or message at no extra charge.

Luath Press Limited
543/2 Castlehill
The Royal Mile
Edinburgh EH1 2ND
Scotland
Telephone: 0131 225 4326 (24 hours)
Fax: 0131 225 4324
email: sales@luath.co.uk
Website: www.luath.co.uk